ZAPIRO
RamApocalypse Now

Cartoons from *Daily Maverick*

Acknowledgements: Thanks to my ever-supportive editors at Daily Maverick (Branko Brkic, Heather Robertson and Marianne Thamm) and to ever-available DM production staff; thanks also to The Annual team (Mike Wills, Eleanora Bresler, Bridget Impey and all at Jacana); cover fundis Roberto Millan and Vanessa Klein; and thanks as always to my family

10 Orange Street
Sunnyside
Auckland Park 2092
South Africa
(+27 11) 628 3200
www.jacana.co.za

in association with

© Jonathan Shapiro, 2023

All rights reserved.

ISBN 978-1-4314-3421-3

Cover design by Jonathan Shapiro
Job no. 004082
Printed and bound by ABC Press, Cape Town

See a complete list of Jacana titles at www.jacana.co.za
See Zapiro's list and archive at www.zapiro.com

For Odette

ZAPIRO annuals

The Madiba Years (1996)
The Hole Truth (1997)
End of Part One (1998)
Call Mr Delivery (1999)
The Devil Made Me Do It! (2000)
The ANC Went in 4x4 (2001)
Bushwhacked (2002)
Dr Do-Little and the African Potato (2003)
Long Walk to Free Time (2004)
Is There a Spin Doctor In the House? (2005)
Da Zuma Code (2006)
Take Two Veg and Call Me In the Morning (2007)
Pirates of Polokwane (2008)
Don't Mess With the President's Head (2009)
Do You Know Who I Am?! (2010)
The Last Sushi (2011)
But Will It Stand Up In Court? (2012)
My Big Fat Gupta Wedding (2013)
It's Code Red! (2014)
Rhodes Rage (2015)
Dead President Walking (2016)
Hasta la Gupta, baby! (2017)
Let the Sunshine In (2018)
Which Side Is Up? (2019)
Do the Macorona (2020)
It Only Comes in Orange, Mr Zuma (2021)
It's Not How It Looks! (2022)

Other books

The Mandela Files (2008)
VuvuzelaNation (2013)
DemoCrazy (2014)
WTF: capturing Zuma – a cartoonist's tale (2018)

23 September 2022

Even Eskom's relentless loadshedding cannot shift mineral resources and energy minister Gwede Mantashe's stubborn investment in coal

Three months before the ANC's elective conference, party elder Kgalema Motlanthe makes a futile plea for an end to premature pronouncements on leadership candidates

Former DA leader Mmusi Maimane's new organisation sounds a lot like that infamous State Capture company of the Watson brothers and convicted crook Angelo Agrizzi

1 October 2022

The party that constantly trumpets renewal is shielding President Cyril Ramaphosa from parliamentary scrutiny of his Phala Phala game farm dealings

5 October 2022

NOBEL SEASON: JACOB ZUMA WINS ALL SIX!!

MEDICINE: for his MIRACULOUS RECOVERY from TERMINAL ILLNESS!!

CHEMISTRY: for his MIRACULOUS RECOVERY from NOVICHOK POISONING by Wife number 3!!

ECONOMICS: for miraculous economic recovery, BANKRUPTCY to HALF A MILLION in ONE DAY!! (courtesy of gangsta crony)

LITERATURE: for the MONUMENTAL LEGAL FICTION in which he prosecutes his prosecutor and that pesky reporter woman!!

PHYSICS: for his unique ability to TURN THE KNOWN UNIVERSE ON ITS HEAD!!

PEACE: HA HA HA HA HA HA HA HAHA!!!

His latest stunt: an outlandish legal action (funded by a crooked diamond dealer) against prosecutor Billy Downer and News24 journalist Karyn Maughan

12 October 2022

14 October 2022 — Utility fees raised sharply as cabinet ministers get free services in state housing

Vainglorious former chief justice says he has been called to become president.
He is promptly endorsed by a previously unknown group.

18 October 2022

21 October 2022

Finally, some action (by the Reserve Bank) against notorious Steinhoff fraudster and mainstay of the horse racing industry, Markus Jooste

26 October 2022 — Cyril says he'll implement Zondo Commission findings. Yeah, sure.

Liz Truss resigns after six calamitous weeks as UK prime minister.
Rishi Sunak becomes the country's fifth leader in seven years.

1 November 2022

3 November 2022

In the wake of a complex saga, Pretoria boy Elon Musk overpays big time for Twitter

Respected amaBhungane investigative journalist Sam Sole trashed by tourism minister and wannabe ANC leader Lindiwe Sisulu following a report on her relationship with her legal adviser

6 November 2022

After nearly four years in the job, National Prosecuting Authority head Shamila Batohi gives a rare interview

North West government spends R800k on faulty donkey carts for rural villagers to get to clinics and schools. The registered supplier knows nothing about the contract.

17 November 2022

20 November 2022 Tainted 2022 FIFA World Cup begins in Qatar

24 November 2022

Loadshedding crisis deepens while Cyril jets off to become King Charles's first state guest

More pitbull horrors. Two young boys killed in separate incidents in the Free State.

26 November 2022

Umpteenth delay and appeal – Western Cape judge president John Hlophe dodges Judicial Service Commission impeachment for improperly trying to influence Constitutional Court judges in a Zuma case 14 years ago

30 November 2022

1 December 2022

Pressure on the president to step down as an
independent panel headed by a former chief justice
finds he has an impeachment case to answer for Phala Phala

Everything hangs on one small word, his backers saying the independent panel report is not conclusive

A cluster of compromised rivals – Gauteng heavyweight Paul Mashatile, sacked health minister Zweli Mkhize, shady deputy president DD Mabuza and loose cannon minister Lindiwe Sisulu – wait for the fall

7 December 2022

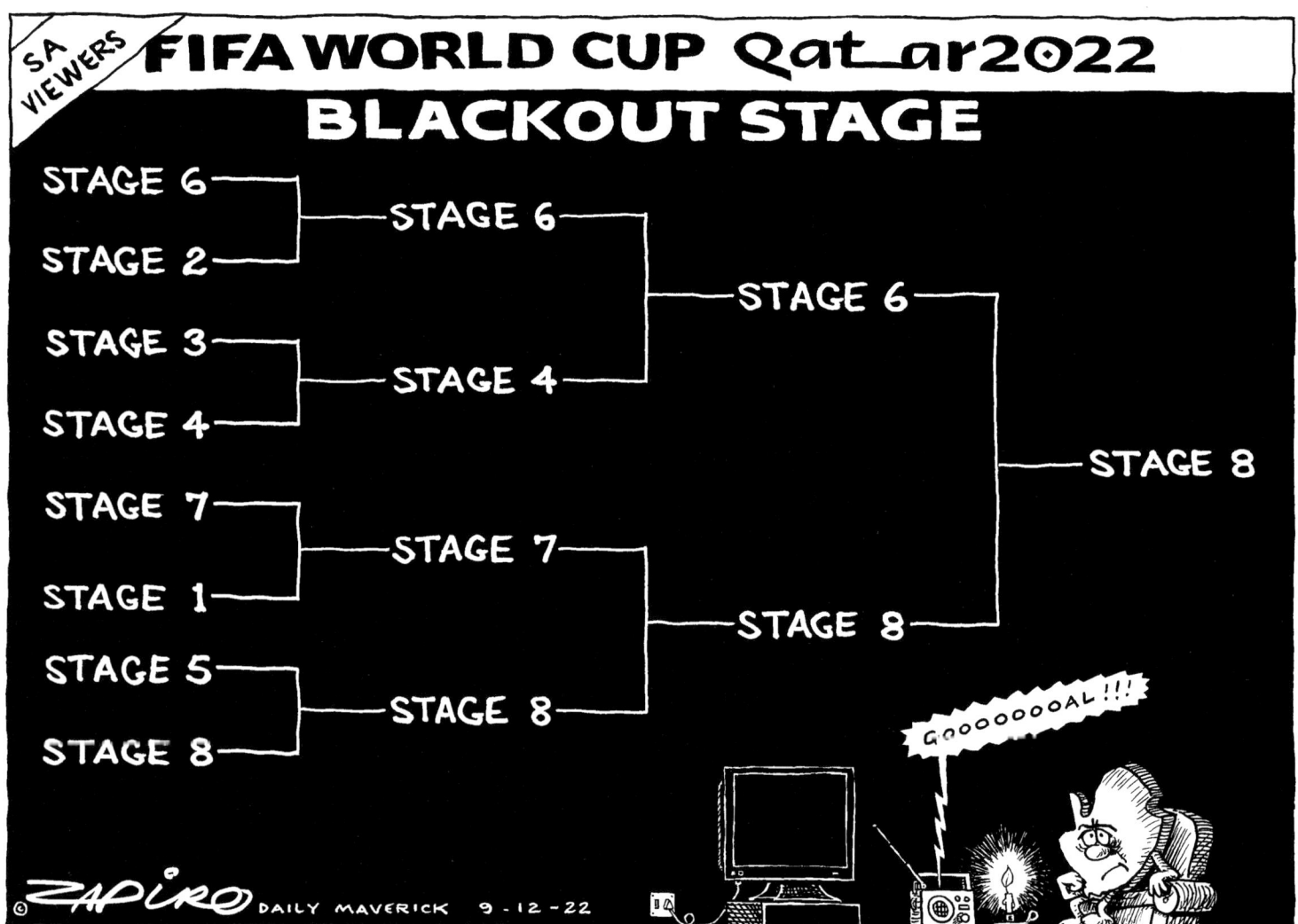

9 December 2022 — Eskom escalates loadshedding stages while we're trying to watch the World Cup

14 December 2022

After three turbulent years in the hotseat and a palpable lack of support from government, André de Ruyter resigns as Eskom CEO

16 December 2022

9 January 2023 — Reluctant president has survived his party conference

A year after Babita Deokaran was killed for reporting massive hospital tender fraud, De Ruyter claims someone tried to poison him for exposing institutionalised Eskom corruption. Looks like the work of State Capture crooks aligned with Zuma's Radical Economic Transformation crew.

11 January 2023

18 January 2023

20 January 2023 Now Gwede Mantashe claims loadshedding can be fixed in six months

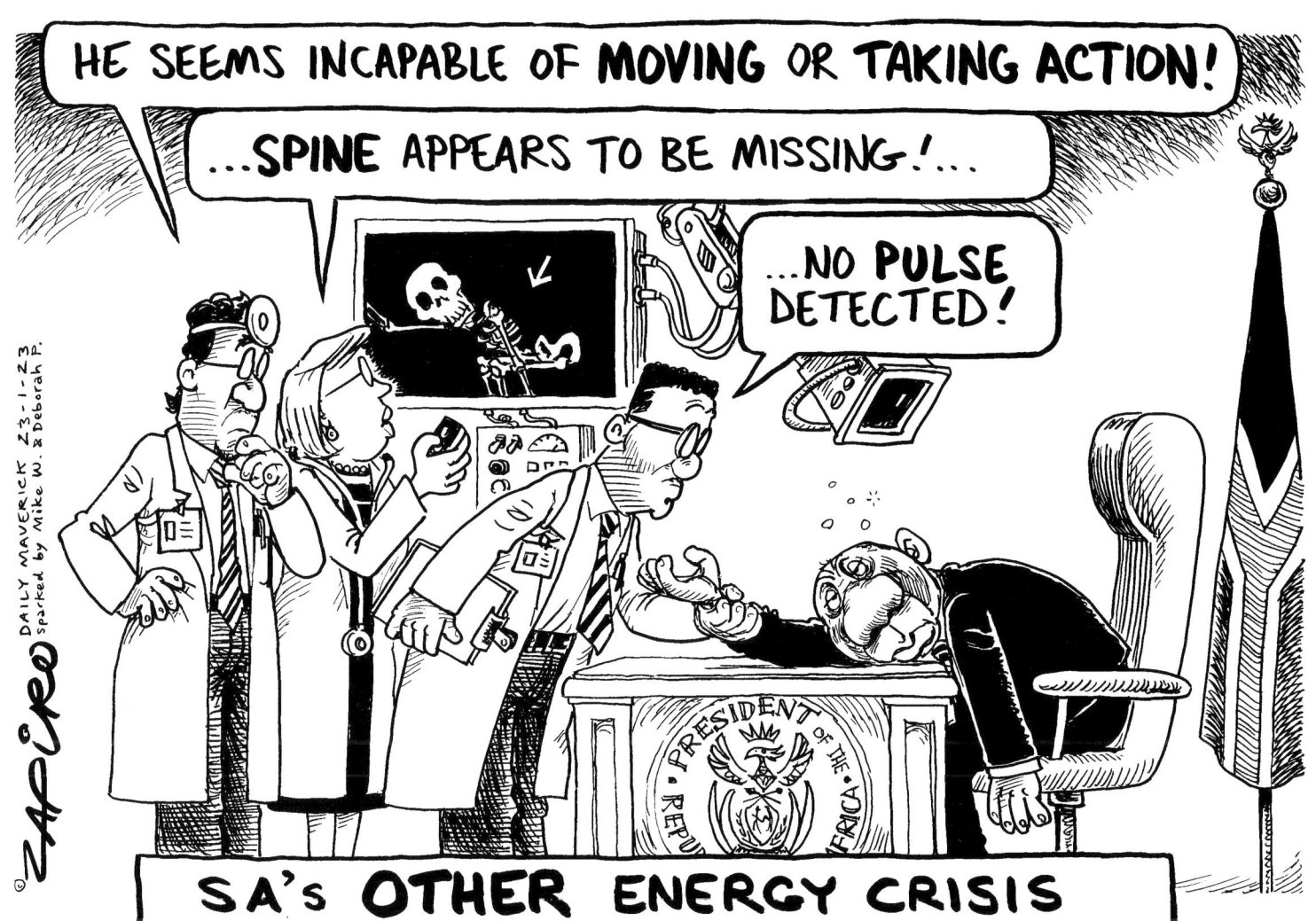

SA plans joint military exercises with the Russians. International relations minister Naledi Pandor meets her counterpart Sergey Lavrov and says calling for a withdrawal from Ukraine is 'simplistic and infantile'.

Minister Sisulu backs a profligate shirt sleeve sponsorship deal for SA Tourism with English Premier League football club Tottenham Hotspur

Mantashe champions exorbitant Turkish ship-mounted gas power plants in the face of widespread criticism of the project

27 January 2023

7 February 2023 — Demands grow for extensive changes in the compromised and ineffective executive

8 February 2023 — Time for the annual presidential State of the Nation song and dance

10 February 2023 — Cyril declares a State of Disaster over Eskom

Filthy rich inheritor of apartheid mining millions touts himself as an outspoken political commentator

16 February 2023 — ANC paints itself as victim of State Capture and claims to lead the charge against it

20 February 2023 — Those provocative military exercises begin off the East Coast

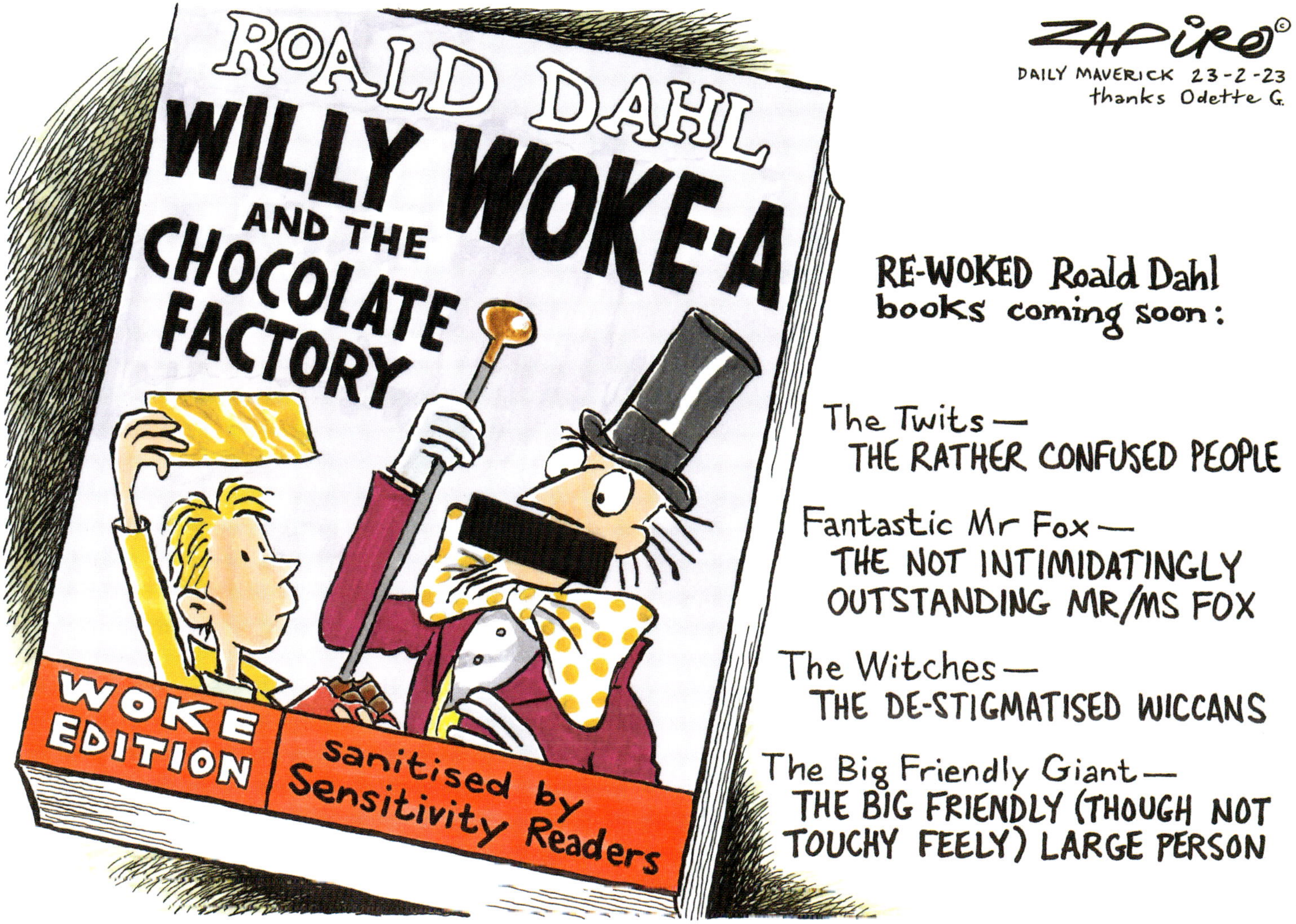

23 February 2023 — Classic children's book edited to remove potentially offensive language

ANC savages De Ruyter when he claims in an explosive TV interview that Eskom is a feeding trough for the party

25 February 2023

Instead of streamlining political responsibility for Eskom, the president comes up with an odd new ministry

28 February 2023

Report in *Daily Maverick* details how criminal syndicates with political links are still looting Eskom

3 March 2023 — Five years of invisibility. Now the crafty deputy president quietly resigns.

8 March 2023 — With yet more ministers and the dead wood staying, the much-delayed reshuffle underwhelms

Former Tshwane mayor Sputla Ramakgopa draws the short straw

Suspended public protector Busisiwe Mkhwebane's lawyer, Dali Mpofu, summons former protector Thuli Madonsela to give evidence and treats her appallingly. She delivers a withering response.

11 March 2023

14 March 2023

Julius Malema's Economic Freedom Fighters call for a national shutdown, demanding 'electricity and the resignation of Ramaphosa'

18 March 2023

21 March 2023 — Much-hyped protest gains little support

23 March 2023 — 25-year-old constitution under the spotlight at a special conference

27 March 2023

Former US president Donald Trump charged with fraud over hush-money payments to porn star Stormy Daniels

6 April 2023 — Trump appears in court – the first president ever to face criminal charges

30 March 2023

Revelations about Facebook rapist and murderer Thabo Bester's bizarre escape from prison just when the International Criminal Court wants Russian president Vladimir Putin detained if he comes to SA for the planned BRICS summit

14 April 2023

Bester's brazen abuse of the prison system only came to light thanks to gutsy investigative media group GroundUp

1 April 2023

John Steenhuisen re-elected as DA leader after defeating Mpho Phalatse while Helen Zille is unopposed as party chairperson

Photoshopped image of the pontiff in a puffer jacket goes viral.
On video, the Dalai Lama asks a young boy to suck his tongue.

12 April 2023

New electricity minister wants to keep coal-fired Eskom units running longer in spite of their inefficiencies and of SA's international commitments to greener energy

Jooste claims passport restrictions mean he cannot appear for his criminal trial in Germany

24 April 2023

UAE ruler pays for an upgrade to Bhisho airport so he and his huge entourage can bypass normal protocol and fly directly to his game farm near Makhanda

Yet another Johannesburg Council coalition pact falls apart as the neophyte minority party mayor announces a mysterious R9.5bn loan to the city which no one knows anything about

26 April 2023

Nonentity Al Jama-ah councillor Kabelo Gwamanda is the new city boss

SA cravenly abstains as even BRICS allies China, India and Brazil vote for a UN resolution describing Russia as the aggressor against Ukraine

4 May 2023

King Charles III is crowned

Zuma spokesperson and former Gupta media owner Mzwanele Manyi dumps the African Transformation Movement and joins the EFF

US Ambassador Reuben Brigety sparks a diplomatic crisis by asserting that SA had sent arms to the Russians in a secretive shipment on the 'Lady R' out of Simonstown five months earlier

12 May 2023

Fears of US sanctions against SA because of the shipment

DA leader announces his 'Moonshot Pact' – an ambitious plan to form a ruling coalition without the ANC or the EFF. Some of the parties named promptly distance themselves because he assumes he'll be in charge.

19 May 2023

Unknown to the publishers, an 'unauthorised' biography of Action SA leader Herman Mashaba by political commentator Prince Mashele had been extensively funded by Mashaba

24 May 2023

26 May 2023

Municipal corruption and shoddy maintenance blamed for an outbreak of cholera in Gauteng which claims more than 30 lives

Providing no details or evidence, defence minister Thandi Modise states in parliament 'we put fokol' on the Lady R

South Africa formally grants Putin diplomatic immunity if he attends the BRICS summit scheduled for Joburg in late August

1 June 2023

Child Protection Week comes and goes

High Court rules that Zuma abused court processes by privately prosecuting advocate Billy Downer and News24 journalist Karyn Maughan. He is ordered to pay their legal fees.

Disgraced ANC heavyweight Ace Magashule permanently expelled by the party after he's found guilty of contravening its constitution

Suspended public protector and her lawyer are shamelessly delaying parliament's impeachment process until her due departure date – three months away – to ensure a hefty payout.

16 June 2023

Despite Ramaphosa's appeasement of Putin, Russian missiles strike Kyiv while he's there to meet Ukrainian President Volodymyr Zelensky

A massive search operation has not yet found any trace of a submersible containing wealthy tourists who had gone to view the world's most famous shipwreck

21 June 2023

26 June 2023 — One year after his final report, chief justice Raymond Zondo damns parliament's inaction

High drama in Russia as Putin ally and Wagner mercenary group boss
Yevgeny Prigozhin launches a rebellion, then suddenly backs down

Turns out ANC secretary general Fikile Mbalula got a R3m housing loan via a crooked former lottery boss; and deputy president Paul Mashatile regularly stays in a luxury residence owned by a State Capture accused.

1 July 2023

Horrific viral video shows Mashatile's VIP armed protection unit viciously assaulting three citizens beside a Gauteng highway

Serious questions about the legality of the dollars stolen from Phala Phala remain unanswered as acting public protector Kholeka Gcaleka clears the president in terms of the Executive Members' Ethics Act

7 July 2023

More mischief from an increasingly desperate Busisiwe Mkhwebane.
She alleges that recently deceased ANC MP Tina Joemat-Pettersson solicited bribes
from her on behalf of cadres including the committee chair of her impeachment hearings.

10 July 2023

July 2021 riots replay? Widespread burning of trucks in KZN.
Police minister says the events are not connected.

Alignment with Russia jeopardises our inclusion in America's African Growth and Opportunity Act, which provides trade benefits

20-year-old Carlos Alcaraz beats veteran
Novak Djokovic in a thrilling Wimbledon final

19 July 2023

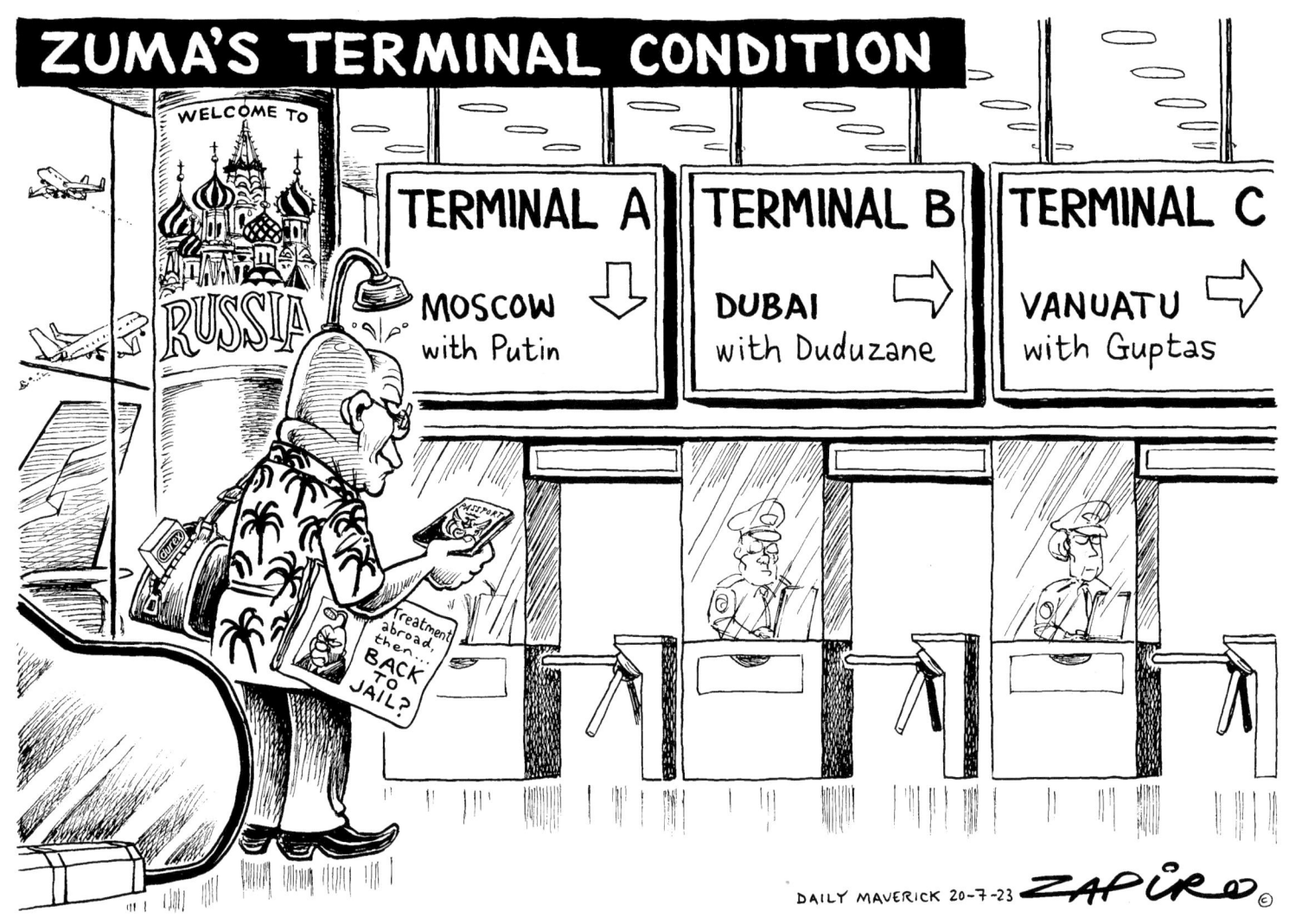

Court rulings that his release from jail was unlawful don't stop Zuma jetting off to Russia for medical treatment

20 July 2023

No one takes responsibility for the explosion that rips up
a central Joburg street, leaving one dead and scores injured

23 July 2023

Russian authorities revoke *Daily Maverick* correspondent's accreditation for Putin's showpiece African summit

His protection unit in the dock as Mashatile changes his story

31 July 2023

The EFF goes large on its tenth anniversary

Banyana Banyana beat Italy 3-2 in the FIFA Women's World Cup, advancing to the knockout stages – a first for any SA team, men or women

2 August 2023

4 August 2023 — Over 100 CEOs pledge to assist government in getting the economy back on track

Cape Town's taxi industry launches a sudden and violent strike after vehicles are impounded. The mayoral committee's security honcho makes matters worse.

10 August 2023

Unappreciated in his home country but a legend in South Africa, American Cold Fact singer Rodriguez dies at 81

The president, justice minister Ronald Lamola and prisons boss Makgothi Thobakgale cook up a remission scheme for thousands of prisoners as a pretext for Zuma to go back to jail for only one hour before being released again

13 August 2023

15 August 2023 — Government talks big on the state of the nation's roads

MARIKANA MASSACRE, 16 AUGUST 2012

11 seconds for heavily armed police to shoot 17 miners dead (and wound 78 others)

11 minutes for police to hunt down and murder in cold blood another 17 miners hiding among nearby rocks

11 years ...and not a single police perpetrator, top brass or politician prosecuted

16 August 2023

Uncomfortable birthday for a key struggle organisation

24 August 2023   China's President Xi calls the shots at the BRICS summit hosted by SA without Putin

Trump's angry mugshot is everywhere after he's charged with illegally interfering in the 2020 US ballot. Zim president Emmerson 'The Crocodile' Mnangagwa claims another fair and square election win for his ruling party.

28 August 2023

30 August 2023 — Acting public protector gets ruling party backing to succeed Busisiwe Mkhwebane

ANC discard Magashule launches his African Congress for Transformation party with equally disgraced former Hawks boss Berning Ntlemeza as a sidekick

Joburg's next disaster. More than 70 die when fire rages through a run-down city centre apartment block, one of many 'hijacked' by criminal gangs.

8 September 2023 — Legendary retailer passes on

12 September 2023

Notoriously verbose and divisive Zulu leader and Inkatha Freedom Party founder dies at 95

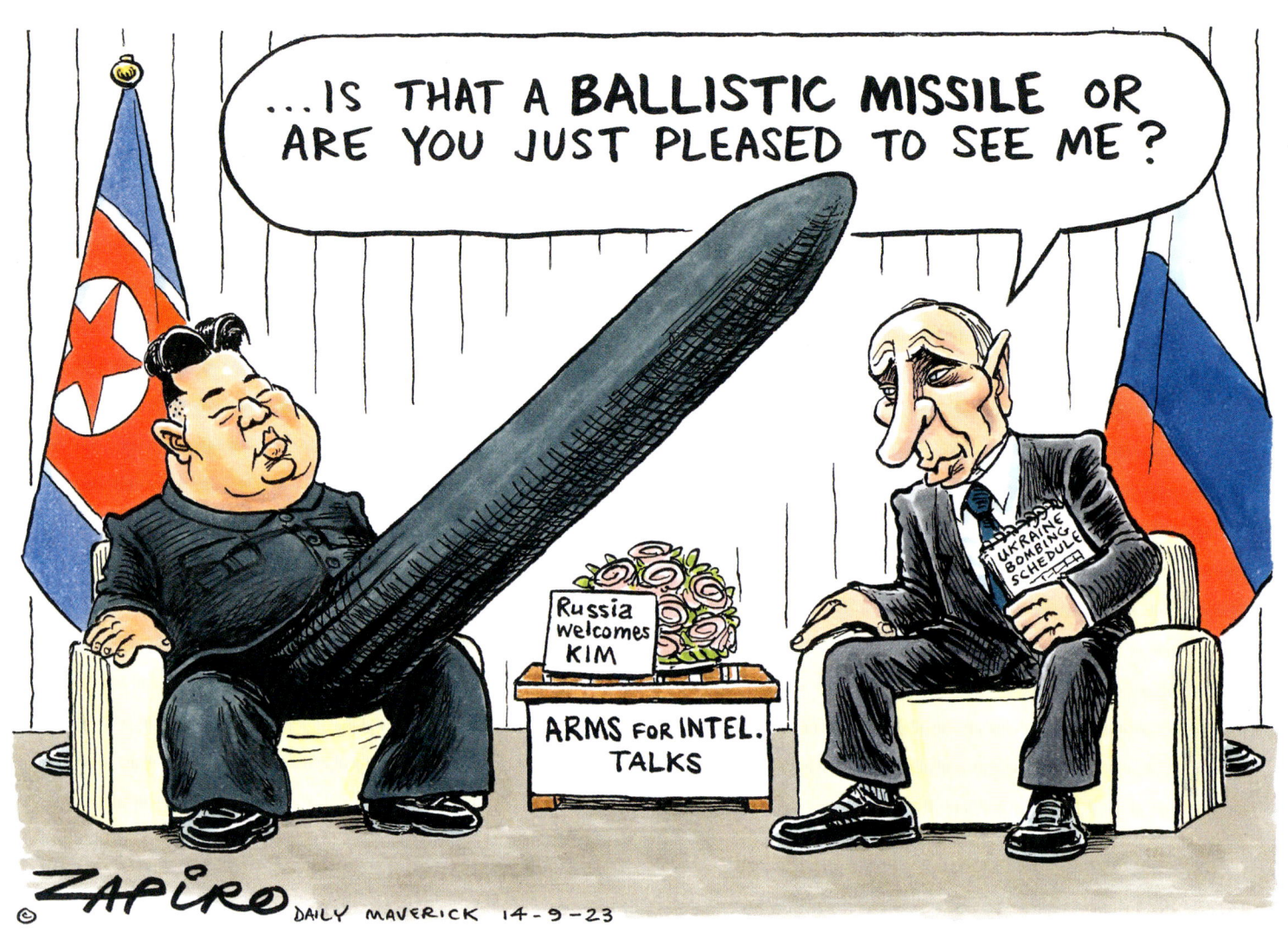

14 September 2023

Running low on allies and weapons, Putin hosts renegade North Korean dictator Kim Jong-un